LIZ LANDRY

From Survival to Surrender

Finding Peace, Releasing Control, Renewing Your Thoughts

To every woman who has ever carried more than she could say,
who has fought silent battles in her mind,
and who has prayed for peace in the quiet hours of the night,
this book is for you.

To the daughters, mothers, sisters, and friends
who love deeply, give freely, and show up bravely
even when your heart feels tired,
may you find rest here.

And to the God who meets us gently,
who renews us daily,
and who never leaves us to carry life alone,
this book is my offering back to You.

Contents

Foreword

Dear Reader,

If this book has found its way into your hands, I believe it's because God is gently inviting you into something new. Maybe into a season of rest. Maybe into a deeper trust. Maybe into a healing you didn't even know you needed. Or maybe into the simple, quiet realization that you don't have to carry life the way you've been carrying it.

You are not reading these pages by coincidence.
There is purpose in your turning here.

There comes a point in every woman's life when the weight she's been holding becomes too heavy to ignore. Not because she's weak, but because she was never meant to carry it alone. And if you're holding this book, I suspect you've reached that moment, the moment your heart whispers, "There has to be a better way to live."

There is.
And that is what this book will lead you toward.

Inside these chapters, you won't be met with pressure to do more, be more, or fix everything you think is broken. Instead, you'll find an invitation, to slow down, to breathe, to surrender, and to rediscover the peace God has been waiting to give you.

This is not a self-help book.
    This is a surrender book.
    A renewal book.
    A transformation-from-the-inside-out book.

You'll explore the patterns that have shaped your thoughts, the fears that have whispered too loudly, the control you've tried to maintain, and the peace that has felt out of reach. But you'll do it gently, with Scripture guiding you and God's presence surrounding you.

I can promise you this:
    You will not walk out of these pages the same woman who walked in.

Not because life will magically change around you, but because something will change within you, in your mind, your spirit, your perspective, and your peace.

So take your time.
    Move through this book slowly.
    Let God speak to you through the sentences that settle in your heart.
    Highlight what resonates, return to what stirs something in you, and allow yourself to be transformed in the process.

God is already here, in the pages ahead.
    And He is already at work in you.

May this book meet you gently.

May it strengthen you quietly.

May it guide you into the peace you've been longing for.

And may you know, deeply and surely, that God is renewing your mind one surrendered moment at a time.

Welcome to the journey.

I'm honored to walk it with you.

Scripture Page

"Do not be conformed to this world, but be transformed by the renewing of your mind..."
    Romans 12:2 (ESV)

"You will keep in perfect peace those whose minds are steadfast, because they trust in You."
    Isaiah 26:3 (NIV)

"Come to Me, all you who are weary and burdened, and I will give you rest."
    Matthew 11:28 (NIV)

"Cast all your anxiety on Him because He cares for you."
    1 Peter 5:7 (NIV)

"For God has not given us a spirit of fear, but of power and of love and of a sound mind."
    2 Timothy 1:7 (NKJV)

"The Lord is close to the brokenhearted and saves those who are crushed in spirit."
    Psalm 34:18 (NIV)

"Trust in the Lord with all your heart and lean not on your own

understanding."
　Proverbs 3:5 (NIV)

Introduction

There comes a moment in every woman's life when she realizes she's tired, not just physically, but mentally, emotionally, and spiritually. Tired of carrying too much. Tired of pretending everything is fine. Tired of surviving when she longs to actually live. Tired of being strong in ways she was never meant to be.

I know that moment well, because I lived there longer than I'd like to admit.

For years, my mind stayed full even when my hands were still. I carried tomorrow's fears, yesterday's regrets, and today's responsibilities all at once. I prayed for peace, but my thoughts raced faster than my faith. I wanted to trust God, but I didn't know how to let go of the things I couldn't control.

Maybe you're reading this book because you've felt the same.

Maybe your mind has been crowded.
   Maybe anxiety has become your normal.
   Maybe you've tried to be everything for everyone.
   Maybe you've forgotten what it feels like to breathe without pressure.

If so, you are exactly where you need to be.

This book is not about becoming a perfect woman with perfect thoughts and a perfectly peaceful life. It's about becoming a renewed woman, one who understands that peace doesn't come from having a calm life, but from having a surrendered mind.

God did not create you to live exhausted.
　He did not design you to be overwhelmed.
　He did not ask you to carry the weight of the world.

He created you to walk with Him, lightly, closely, daily.

The journey you're about to begin is not a quick fix or a motivational pep talk. It's a transformation. A spiritual, emotional, and mental shift from surviving to surrendering, from spiraling thoughts to steady truth, from fear-filled thinking to faith-filled living.

In these chapters, you will learn how to:

release what you were never meant to hold,

rest in God's presence instead of pressure,

renew your thoughts with His truth,

rewrite the words you speak over yourself,

reframe your hardest seasons, and

rise into the woman God designed you to be.

And you'll do it one gentle step at a time.

You don't have to rush this process.
    You don't have to master it overnight.
    You don't have to feel strong to begin.

You just have to be willing.

Willing to trust God with the things you've carried.
    Willing to let Him reshape the thoughts that have shaped your life.
    Willing to believe that peace is possible for you, not someday, but now.

As you read, I invite you to be honest with yourself.
    Give yourself permission to slow down.
    Let these words sit with you.
    Highlight, underline, breathe, and let God speak.

Your mind is not broken.
    Your heart is not too heavy.
    Your story is not too complicated.
    Your peace is not out of reach.

You are stepping into a new chapter, one where you don't have to live overwhelmed anymore. One where God meets you gently, renews you daily, and leads you into a life marked by peace.

Welcome to the journey of renewal, freedom, and surrender.

You're not here by accident.

God led you.

And He's going to walk with you every step of the way.

Let's begin.

1

Weight — The Thoughts That Are Too Heavy to Carry

"Come to Me, all who are weary and burdened, and I will give you rest."
— Matthew 11:28 (NIV)

Some weights don't live on your shoulders; they live in your thoughts.

The heaviness you feel isn't always physical; sometimes it's the quiet pressure of worries, expectations, memories, and fears that pile up in the mind until you're moving through life with an invisible load no one else can see.

You've been carrying the day before it even begins.

You've been holding more than your heart was built to handle.

And somewhere deep inside, your mind is whispering, *"This is too much."*

This chapter is an invitation to finally acknowledge that weight, and to release what was never yours to carry.

There are seasons in a woman's life where the weight she

carries is not visible to anyone else, but she feels it in every breath. Not in her shoulders or her hands, but in her *mind*. A heaviness that settles quietly, quietly enough that others may never notice, yet loud enough inside that she can't escape it.

It's the weight of overthinking.

The weight of worrying too early.

The weight of replaying conversations in her head.

The weight of preparing for things that may never even happen.

The weight of being strong for everyone else.

The weight of silently carrying what she doesn't know how to put down.

Women don't always break down physically.

But their minds get tired, deeply tired, long before their bodies ever do.

Maybe that's you.

Maybe your mind has been running even when your body is still.

Maybe the invisible load you're carrying feels heavier than anything anyone can see.

Maybe you've held it together for so long that even letting yourself fall apart feels impossible.

You're not imagining that weight.

You're not "too emotional."

You're not weak.

You're not dramatic.

You're a woman who has been carrying far too much for far too long.

And here's the truth no one ever told you:

You were never created to live with that much weight in your mind.

When the Mind Becomes a Backpack

Imagine your mind like a backpack.

Every thought, every fear, every responsibility, every "what if," every disappointment, every burden becomes another item thrown inside. Not one at a time, but all at once.

At first, you can carry it.

You can walk.

You can function.

You can smile.

You can still show up for others.

But then, one day, you pick it up and realize the straps are cutting into your shoulders. The weight is pressing into your back. The load is making you bend. And suddenly the simple act of walking, mentally, emotionally, spiritually, feels heavier than it should.

That's because it *is* heavier than it should be.

Jesus didn't ask you to carry the load of your life.

He didn't ask you to hold onto pressures that crush your peace.

He didn't ask you to drag unspoken fears through every day.

He said the opposite:

"Come to Me, all you who are weary and burdened, and I will give you rest."

— Matthew 11:28

Weary.

Burdened.

Heavy.

He named your condition before you even learned how to describe it.

7

The Heavy Thoughts God Never Intended You to Carry

Here are some weights God never meant for you to hold:

- *The weight of future outcomes*

"Will it work out? What will happen next? How will this all end?"

- *The weight of other people's emotions*

"I need to keep them happy."
  "I need to fix what they're feeling."
  "I need to hold their world together."

- *The weight of perfection*

"I can't get this wrong."
  "I can't disappoint anyone."
  "I have to be strong."

- *The weight of past mistakes*

The regrets you replay.
  The moments you wish you could undo.
  The shame you secretly carry.

● *The weight of unspoken fear*

Fear of losing someone.
Fear of being alone.
Fear of being misunderstood.
Fear of falling short.
God did not call you to carry any of these, but life trained you to.
That's why the first step of your healing isn't "trying harder."
It's simply recognizing that **you're carrying things you were never built to hold.**

What Happens When the Mind Grows Heavy

You feel it in subtle ways:

- You wake up tired even after sleeping.
- You overthink every small choice.
- You feel anxious without knowing why.
- You withdraw emotionally.
- You feel overwhelmed by simple decisions.
- You carry everyone's feelings as if they're your responsibility.
- You feel guilty for needing a break.
- You're functioning, but not fully living.

This is the mind signaling:
"I wasn't meant to carry this weight alone."
In Scripture, God continually warns His people about carrying burdens that belong to Him:

"Cast your burden on the Lord, and He will sustain you."

— Psalm 55:22

"Cast all your anxiety on Him because He cares for you."

— 1 Peter 5:7

Why does God repeat it?

Because He knows women tend to carry things He never asked them to carry.

The Quiet Truth:

Survival mode is not the way God intends for you to live.

Survival is loud.

Surrender is peaceful.

Survival is heavy.

Surrender is freeing.

Survival depends on your strength.

Surrender depends on His.

Before we go anywhere else in this book, we need to say this clearly:

Not everything your mind is carrying belongs to you.

And the beautiful thing about God is this:

He doesn't shame you for picking up the weight.

He just invites you to put it down.

A Truth to Hold Onto

You don't have to carry the weight of your thoughts.
  God is strong enough to carry what has been breaking you.

Closing Prayer

Lord, I bring You the weight I've been carrying, the worries I haven't spoken, the fears I haven't expressed, and the thoughts that have grown too heavy for me to manage on my own. Help me recognize what is mine to carry and what I need to release. Teach me to trust You with the burdens that were never meant for my shoulders. Lighten my mind, calm my spirit, and lead me into Your peace. In Jesus' name, amen.

2

Lies — The Thoughts That Distort the Truth

If the enemy cannot destroy you, he will distract you.

If he cannot defeat you, he will deceive you.

If he cannot take your life, he will target your mind.

And he does it with lies.

Not loud lies.

Not obvious lies.

But quiet ones, whispered in the moments you're tired, overwhelmed, unsure, or alone. The kind of lies that slip so subtly into your thoughts that you begin repeating them to yourself without realizing they never came from God.

Every heavy thought has a root.

Every anxious spiral has a starting point.

Every controlling pattern begins with a small lie you believed before you even knew you were believing it.

This chapter is about identifying the lies that quietly, persistently shape your reality, and learning to replace them with God's truth.

The Enemy Works in Whispers

The enemy rarely shouts at you.
   He whispers.
   He whispers when you're tired.
   He whispers when you feel alone.
   He whispers when you fail.
   He whispers when you're afraid.
   He whispers when you don't understand what God is doing.
   He whispers:
   "You're not enough."
   "You're doing everything wrong."
   "You're falling behind."
   "You always mess things up."
   "No one understands you."
   "Things will never change."
   "You aren't strong enough for this."
   "You have to fix everything yourself."
   These whispers are strategic.
   They sound like your own thoughts.
   They sound reasonable.
   They sound familiar.
   But they are lies.
   And here's the dangerous part:
   A lie you hear enough times eventually sounds like truth.

The First Lie Women Believe: "I Should Be Stronger Than This."

This lie is almost universal.

Women believe they must carry more without breaking, without resting, without needing help, without slowing down. And when they start to feel overwhelmed, they don't admit it, they shame themselves for it.

But God never asked you to be strong without Him.

Scripture tells us:

"My grace is sufficient for you, for My power is made perfect in weakness."

— 2 Corinthians 12:9

Weakness is not the problem.

Shame around weakness is.

Your weakness is where God shows up.

Your weakness is where He strengthens you.

Your weakness is where His Spirit takes over.

The lie says:

"You should be stronger."

God says:

"Let Me be your strength."

The Second Lie: "I'm Alone in What I'm Feeling."

One of the enemy's favorite tactics is isolation.

If he can convince you that you're the only one struggling, you won't reach out, you won't pray honestly, and you won't pursue healing. You'll keep pretending you're fine while your soul grows tired.

But Scripture says:

"The Lord is close to the brokenhearted."

— Psalm 34:18

Close.

Not distant.

Not watching from afar.

Not waiting for you to get it together.

Close.

And you're not the only woman who feels this way.

Your struggle is not strange; it's human.

Nothing you feel disqualifies you from God's love or His healing.

The Third Lie: "Things Will Always Be This Way."

This lie makes you hopeless.

Hopelessness makes you heavy.

And heaviness makes you surrender to survival.

The enemy wants you to believe you'll always overthink, you'll always worry, you'll always spiral, you'll always be anxious, you'll always fear the worst.

But God says:

"I am doing a new thing... do you not perceive it?"

— Isaiah 43:19

New.

Not repeated.

Not recycled.
Not the same as before.
Your story is not stuck.
Your mind is not stuck.
Your situation is not stuck.
God is already moving in ways you cannot yet see.

The Fourth Lie: "Peace Is Not Possible for Me."

Many women believe peace is real, just not for *them*.
    They believe other people can experience it, but not someone with their history, their anxiety, their burdens, their life.
    But Jesus said:

"Peace I leave with you; My peace I give you."

— John 14:27
    Not peace for the perfect.
    Not peace for the calm.
    Not peace for those who have everything figured out.
    Peace for you.
    Peace is not earned.
    Peace is received.

Lies Shape You — Until Truth Sets You Free

The enemy lies to you for one reason:
    If he can control your thoughts, he can control your life.
    But God's Word does the exact opposite.
    It sets you free.
    Jesus said:

"You will know the truth, and the truth will set you free."

— John 8:32

Truth destroys the power of lies.
Truth lifts the weight they created.
Truth breaks the cycles you've been stuck in.
But to replace a lie, you must first recognize it.

How to Identify a Lie in Your Mind

Ask these three questions:

1. Does this thought align with God's character?

If not, it's not from Him.

2. Does this thought bring fear, shame, or confusion?

God's voice brings conviction, yes, but never condemnation.

3. Would I say this to a friend I love?

If the answer is no, why are you speaking it to yourself?

The Truth You Need Right Now

Here are truths that God wants to root deep in your heart:

- You are not alone.
- You are not failing.
- You are not too much.

- You are not behind.
- You are not forgotten.
- You are not hopeless.
- You are not disqualified.
- You are not broken beyond repair.

You are loved.
  You are seen.
  You are chosen.
  You are capable.
  You are covered.
  You are strengthened by God Himself.

A Truth to Hold Onto

The enemy lies to weaken you.
  God speaks truth to restore you.

You get to choose which voice you believe.

Closing Prayer

Lord, reveal every lie I've been believing, the ones that have shaped my thoughts, my emotions, and my sense of self. Expose the whispers that are not from You. Replace them with Your truth. Let Your Word become louder than fear and clearer than doubt. Help me believe what You say about me, even when my feelings tell a different story. Protect my mind and renew my thoughts. In Jesus' name, amen.

3

Control — When Letting Go Feels Impossible

Have you ever caught yourself planning, managing, predicting, fixing, and anticipating everything around you before you've even had your morning coffee?

You don't mean to control things, it just feels safer to stay ahead of problems than to be surprised by them.

You've carried so much for so long that control doesn't feel like control anymore, it feels like responsibility.

But beneath the urge to manage everything is a deeper truth God is gently calling you to see:

not everything you carry belongs in your hands.

There is a point in every woman's life where she realizes something she doesn't want to admit:

She has been trying to control things that were never in her control to begin with.

Not because she's manipulative.

Not because she's selfish.

Not because she thinks too highly of herself.

But because somewhere along the way, life taught her:
"If you don't hold it together, everything will fall apart."
So she became the problem-solver.
The emotional caretaker.
The one who anticipates needs before anyone speaks.
The one who fixes issues before they escalate.
The one who carries the weight of making sure everyone else is okay, even at the cost of her own peace.
Maybe that's you.
Maybe you don't *want* to control everything, but you feel responsible for everything.
If someone is hurting, you want to heal them.
If someone is struggling, you want to help them.
If someone is upset, you want to calm them.
If someone is distant, you want to fix the relationship.
If someone is unhappy, you want to make it better.
If someone is disappointed, you want to soften the blow.
So you carry the emotional atmosphere of the room.
You carry the weight of everyone's expectations.
You carry the fear of what might happen if you stop managing everything.
But here is the truth you've been avoiding:

Trying to control what you cannot control is the fastest way to exhaust your soul.

Control Is a Response to Fear

You don't control because you're overconfident.

You control because you're terrified of what will happen if you don't.

Control is often rooted in:

- fear of losing people
- fear of being hurt again
- fear of being disappointed
- fear of repeating old patterns
- fear of being blindsided
- fear of not being enough
- fear of not being loved
- fear of everything falling apart
- fear of the unknown

That's why letting go feels unsafe.

That's why surrender feels vulnerable.

That's why trust feels risky.

But here's what God knows that you sometimes forget:

You were never meant to carry fear; you were meant to carry faith.

What Control Looks Like (Even When It's Invisible)

Control isn't always loud or obvious.
Sometimes it looks very quiet, even caring.

- You rehearse conversations in your mind.
- You anticipate everyone's reactions.
- You over-plan to avoid disappointment.
- You keep busy to avoid thinking.
- You hold back emotions to avoid being a burden.
- You check on everyone but yourself.
- You take responsibility for people's feelings.
- You avoid asking for help because you don't want to feel weak.
- You try to manage outcomes as if the weight of the world rests on you.

Control feels like protection, but it's actually a prison.

The Illusion of Control

Control gives the illusion of safety.
It gives the illusion of predictability.
It gives the illusion of stability.
But it is just that, an illusion.
Because no matter how hard you try, you cannot:

- control someone else's choices
- control someone else's healing
- control someone else's emotions
- control someone else's timing

22

- control someone else's growth
- control someone else's love
- control the future
- control outcomes
- control what God is doing behind the scenes

And when you try, you will always end up tired.

Because you're attempting to do God's job with human strength.

What God Says About Control

God is not vague about who holds the world together, and it isn't you.

"Be still, and know that I am God."

— Psalm 46:10
   Stillness is surrender.
   Stillness is trust.
   Stillness is releasing what you were never meant to carry.

"Trust in the Lord with all your heart and lean not on your own understanding."

— Proverbs 3:5
   Your understanding is limited.
   His is endless.

"The heart of man plans his way, but the Lord establishes his steps."

— Proverbs 16:9
   You can plan.
   But you cannot control.
   And that's not a punishment, it's freedom.

The Hardest Truth to Accept

You cannot control everything because you were not created to.
   Your hands were never meant to hold the world; His were.
   But here is the beauty:
   What feels out of your control is fully in God's control.
   What feels chaotic to you is clear to Him.
   What feels overwhelming to you is simple to Him.
   What feels impossible to you is easy for Him.

Surrender Is Not Giving Up — It's Giving Back

Many women think surrender means quitting, losing, or failing.
   But surrender is not a loss, it's a release.
   Surrender says:
   "I don't have to force this."
   "I don't have to fix this."
   "I don't have to figure this out alone."
   "This outcome is not mine to control."
   "God, this belongs to You."
   Surrender is not weakness; it is spiritual strength.

24

What Happens When You Stop Trying to Control Everything

You find breath again.
You find peace again.
You find clarity again.
You find God in the places where fear used to live.
When you release control:

- stress loosens its grip
- anxiety softens
- overthinking quiets
- relationships feel lighter
- you stop carrying emotions that don't belong to you
- you hear God more clearly
- you regain the energy you lost trying to hold everything together

Because surrender is not just a moment, it's a lifestyle.

A Truth to Hold Onto

You don't have to hold everything together.
God is holding you, and everything connected to you.

Closing Prayer

Lord, I confess that I have been carrying things I was never meant to control. I've tried to fix what only You can heal, hold together what only You can sustain, and manage outcomes that belong to You. Teach me to trust You more deeply. Help me release my grip.

Remind me that surrender is not loss, it's freedom. Show me the peace that comes from letting go and letting You lead. In Jesus' name, amen.

4

Release — Giving God What You Were Never Meant to Hold

What would happen if you loosened your grip just a little?

If you stopped holding the outcome, the fear, the tension, the timeline?

If you opened the hand you've kept clenched for years?

Most women don't struggle to release because they're stubborn, they struggle because letting go feels unsafe.

But the very thing you're afraid to release may be the very thing God is asking to heal.

This chapter guides you gently into the freedom of entrusting God with what has been weighing on you.

There is a moment in every woman's healing where she faces a crossroads:

Hold on... or let go.

Not because letting go is easy.

Not because she's suddenly brave.

Not because her situation magically makes sense.

But because she finally realizes something sacred:

What she's been holding onto is holding her back.

Release is the turning point, the moment where survival ends and surrender begins.

But here's the truth:

Release doesn't start in your hands.

Release starts in your *mind*.

You must loosen your thoughts before you can loosen your grip.

Why Releasing Is So Hard

Women hold on for many reasons:

- We want to protect the people we love.
- We fear what will happen if we loosen our control.
- We believe letting go means abandoning responsibility.
- We've learned to depend on ourselves more than others.
- We're afraid that if we stop "managing," something will fall apart.
- We think our involvement guarantees safety, stability, or success.

Letting go feels risky because you don't know how the story will unfold without your hands on it.

But holding on hasn't been giving you peace either.

Holding on has left your mind crowded, your emotions tight, your sleep interrupted, and your heart unsettled.

You're not failing to release —

you're simply scared of what happens if you do.

God knows that.

And that's why He doesn't demand release.

He *invites* it.

What Release Actually Means

Release is not giving up.
Release is not being passive.
Release is not stepping back irresponsibly.
Release is not pretending everything is fine.
Release simply means:
"I'm placing this into God's hands because mine were never meant to carry it."
Release is transferring responsibility
from your shoulders
to God's sovereignty.
Release is an act of trust.
Release is an act of worship.

God Never Intended You to Carry Everything

Scripture makes this beautifully clear:

"Cast your burden on the Lord, and He will sustain you."

— Psalm 55:22
He can sustain you.
He will sustain you.
You were not meant to sustain yourself.

"Give all your worries and cares to God, for He cares about you."

— 1 Peter 5:7

You are not putting your burdens into a void.

You are placing them into the hands of a Father who cares deeply and personally.

"Come to Me, all you who are weary and burdened, and I will give you rest."

— Matthew 11:28

You come carrying weight.

He sends you away with rest.

Release is not one moment.

It is a pattern.

A rhythm.

A daily choice.

Release Happens in Layers

Some things you release once.

Other things you have to release again and again until your mind finally stops returning to them.

Release is not weakness; it is repetition.

Sometimes release looks like:

- writing down the fear and handing it back to God
- saying, "Lord, this is too heavy for me"
- releasing your children into God's care
- releasing the need to fix relationships

- releasing the desire to control outcomes
- releasing the story you thought your life would be
- releasing the future you imagined
- releasing your grip on timelines
- releasing the shame of your past
- releasing the fear of "what if"

Release is not instant.
Release is a journey.

What Happens When You Begin to Release

As you let go, in pieces, in waves, in whispers, you will feel something shift:

- Your anxiety softens.
- Your thoughts lighten.
- Your shoulders loosen.
- Your breathing deepens.
- Your sleep improves.
- Your emotions settle.
- Your reactions slow down.
- Your peace returns.
- Your confidence grows.

Because the moment you place something in God's hands,
    your mind no longer has to carry the weight of what happens next.
    Release restores clarity.
    Release restores trust.
    Release restores your heart.

31

Letting Go Doesn't Mean You Don't Care

Sometimes women resist letting go because they believe:
   "If I release this, it means I don't care."
   No.
   Release is not indifference.
   Release is partnership.
   You are allowing God to do what ONLY God can do.
   You STILL show up.
   You STILL pray.
   You STILL care.
   You STILL take steps of faith.
   But you stop trying to control the outcome.
   You release your grip,
   but you do not release your faith.

What You Need to Release Right Now

Take a deep breath and answer this honestly:
   What has your mind been carrying that your heart cannot handle anymore?
   Is it:

- a relationship you can't fix?
- a child you're worried about?
- a situation you can't control?
- a future you can't predict?
- a decision you're afraid to make?
- an emotion you can't name?
- a fear that's growing louder?
- a burden you've kept private?

· a timeline you're frustrated with?

God is whispering:
"Give it to Me."
Not tomorrow.
Not later.
Not when life feels lighter.
Now.
Here.
In this moment.

A Truth to Hold Onto

Release doesn't remove responsibility.
Release removes the weight of pretending you're God.

Closing Prayer

Lord, I release every burden I've been holding onto, the ones I've spoken aloud and the ones I've kept hidden in my heart. I surrender my fear, my timeline, my expectations, my relationships, and the outcomes I cannot control. Teach me to trust Your strength more than my own. Help me loosen my grip and transfer the weight from my hands into Yours. Show me the peace that comes from releasing what was never meant for me. In Jesus' name, amen.

5

Rest — Living From Peace Instead of Pressure

You can sleep eight hours and still wake up exhausted.

You can take a day off and still feel overwhelmed.

You can pause your schedule and still feel mentally crowded.

That's because true rest has nothing to do with inactivity and everything to do with the condition of your soul.

Rest isn't waiting for life to calm down.

Rest is learning to calm your mind in the presence of God.

This chapter is where you begin to practice the kind of rest that restores you from the inside out.

There comes a point in a woman's life when she realizes she has been moving, thinking, giving, showing up, and pouring out long after her soul ran empty.

Not because she wants to.

Not because she's trying to impress anyone.

Not because she doesn't know better.

But because she has learned to function while tired, and she's been tired for so long that she doesn't even recognize it anymore.

Women are skilled at resting their bodies while their minds keep running.

You can sit down, but your thoughts keep walking.

You can lay in bed, but your mind keeps planning.

You can close your eyes, but your heart keeps bracing for the next thing.

Rest has become a distant, unfamiliar idea, something you hope to experience "one day," when the responsibilities lighten, when things get easier, when the chaos slows down.

But that day never seems to come.

Rest isn't a luxury you earn.

Rest is a *gift* God gives, and it starts in your mind long before it reaches your body.

Rest Isn't the Absence of Activity — It's the Presence of God

Many women believe rest is the same as inactivity:

- taking a nap,
- watching a show,
- sitting quietly,
- taking a break.

Those things help, but they don't heal.

You can stop moving physically and still be exhausted mentally.

Biblical rest is different.

Biblical rest is a spiritual posture where your mind loosens, your heart quiets, and your spirit settles because you trust God

FROM SURVIVAL TO SURRENDER

more than you trust your own strength.
This is the rest Jesus invites you into:

"Come to Me...and I will give you rest."

— Matthew 11:28
Rest is not earned.
Rest is *given*.
Rest is received, not achieved.
You don't rest because everything is calm.
You rest because God is in control.

Rest Begins Where Control Ends

Control keeps you tense.
Release opens the door.
But rest, rest is the moment your soul finally exhales.
Rest is the fruit of surrender.
Rest is the peace that follows release.
Rest is the quiet confidence that God is handling what you cannot.
Rest is where your mind learns:
"I don't have to hold everything.
I don't have to fear tomorrow.
I don't have to understand how everything will work out.
God is already there."
Rest is the inner stillness that settles in when you finally stop micromanaging your life and allow God to be God.

Why Rest Feels Uncomfortable at First

For many women, rest doesn't feel peaceful at the beginning; it feels *foreign*.

You're so used to:

- staying busy
- multitasking
- managing everyone's emotions
- fixing problems before they appear
- anticipating needs
- thinking ahead
- staying "on alert"

that when everything slows down, your mind doesn't know what to do.

Rest feels unsafe when you've survived chaos.

Rest feels strange when your nervous system has lived in overdrive.

Rest feels selfish when you've spent years caring for everyone else.

But here's a truth you must let settle deep within you:

Rest is not selfish; rest is spiritual obedience.

God commanded rest.

God modeled rest.

God blesses rest.

Rest is holy.

God's Gift of Rest Is for You

In Exodus, before God gave His people commandments, He gave them rest.

In Psalm 23, before God leads you into righteousness, He makes you lie down.

"He makes me lie down in green pastures; He leads me beside quiet waters; He restores my soul."

— Psalm 23:2–3

Notice the sequence:

Lie down → Quiet waters → Restoration

Rest is not optional.

Rest is restorative.

Rest is God's method of rebuilding you.

And He wants to rebuild you.

Signs You Need Rest — Deep Soul Rest

Here are signs a woman needs rest at the soul level:

- You wake up tired even after sleeping.
- Your mind jumps straight to problems.
- You feel behind before the day starts.
- You can't stop overthinking small decisions.
- You get irritated easily.
- Your emotions feel fragile.
- You avoid stillness because it feels uncomfortable.
- You feel guilty for wanting a break.
- You cry unexpectedly over small things.

· You constantly feel like you're "on alert."

These aren't signs of weakness.
    They're signs you've been carrying too much.
    And God sees it.

God Invites You Into Rest When You're Overwhelmed

When Elijah felt overwhelmed, God didn't tell him:
    "Get up. Push through. Try harder."
    No.
    God gave him rest.
    He let him sleep.
    He fed him.
    He replenished him.
    He restored him gently.
    Then God whispered.
    Rest comes before revelation.
    Rest comes before strength.
    Rest comes before clarity.
    God does not speak loudly to an exhausted mind
    He speaks softly to a rested one.

How to Practice Rest When Your Mind Doesn't Want to Slow Down

Here are practical, simple, biblical ways to cultivate mental + spiritual rest:

1. Breathe before you respond.

A 3-second breath interrupts anxiety and creates space for calm.

2. Sit with God for 5 quiet minutes.

No agenda. No words. Just stillness.
   Let Him settle your thoughts.

3. Release one thing a day.

You don't have to surrender everything at once.
   Start with one worry.

4. Speak truth over yourself.

"I don't have to carry this alone."
   "God is with me right now."
   "I choose rest instead of fear."

5. Reject the guilt of slowing down.

Jesus rested.
   You can too.

6. Practice sacred simplicity.

Reduce noise.
   Declutter your physical + mental spaces.
   Peace thrives in simplicity.

7. *Protect your boundaries.*

Rest requires emotional space.
   Say no with grace.
   Say yes with intention.

Rest Is Where God Heals What You Didn't Know Was Broken

When your mind finally rests:

- old wounds surface
- hidden fears soften
- emotions you've buried rise
- God reveals lies you've believed
- your heart becomes teachable again
- your spirit becomes quiet enough to hear Him

Rest is not empty.
   Rest is full, full of God's presence, comfort, and clarity.

You Cannot Live Renewed Without Learning to Rest

Rest is God's reset button for your mind.
   Rest prepares you for renewal.
   Rest creates space for truth.
   Rest strengthens your spirit.
   Rest stabilizes your emotions.
   Rest restores your identity.
   Rest protects your peace.
   Rest aligns your heart with God's heart.

Rest is not the end.
Rest is the beginning of transformation.

A Truth to Hold Onto

**Rest is not what you do after everything is fixed —
rest is what helps God fix what you've been carrying.**

Closing Prayer

Lord, teach me to rest. Not just in my body, but in my mind, my spirit, and my heart. Quiet the thoughts that keep running, soften the fears that keep rising, and loosen the burdens that keep returning. Lead me beside Your still waters. Restore my soul where it has grown weary. Help me release guilt, resist busyness, and receive the rest You freely give. In Jesus' name, amen.

6

Renew — Replacing Old Thoughts With God's Truth

The mind is a garden, and every thought is a seed.

Some seeds grow into peace, hope, and clarity.

Others grow into worry, fear, and insecurity.

And for many women, the garden of the mind has been neglected for so long that weeds have taken root in places God intended to flourish.

But here is the grace in it:

God is not intimidated by the condition of your mind.

He specializes in renewal.

Renewal doesn't happen in an instant.

It happens in layers, slowly, consistently, intentionally, as God begins to reshape the way you think, feel, and respond to life.

This chapter is about embracing the tender, powerful work God does when He begins renewing your thoughts from the inside out.

Renewal Begins With Awareness, Not Perfection

Most women assume renewal starts when they finally "get it together."

But renewal actually begins the moment you become aware that your old way of thinking isn't working anymore.

Awareness isn't condemnation.

Awareness is awakening.

Awareness says:

- "This belief isn't helping me."
- "This thought isn't true."
- "This pattern isn't healthy."
- "This reaction isn't from God."
- "This fear doesn't match His promises."

God never condemns awareness, He uses it.

It's the Holy Spirit gently tapping your heart, saying:

"There's more freedom for you than the way you've been living."

Renewal Happens When You Interrupt Old Patterns

The enemy loves patterns.

He thrives in repetition.

If he can keep you thinking the same thoughts, he can keep you feeling the same feelings, and living the same way.

Renewal begins when you interrupt the cycle.

When you stop repeating lies and start replacing them with truth.

When you stop reacting from fear and start responding from faith.

When you stop replaying the past and start rewriting your present.

Even the smallest shift can uproot years of heavy thinking.

What God Says About Renewal

God doesn't hide what He can do with the mind.

He declares it boldly:

"Be transformed by the renewing of your mind."

— Romans 12:2

Transformation doesn't come from trying harder.

Transformation comes from letting God renew the way you think.

"You were taught... to be made new in the attitude of your minds."

— Ephesians 4:23

Not just new habits.

Not just new emotions.

Not just new perspectives.

A new attitude of the mind.

"We take captive every thought to make it obedient to Christ."

— 2 Corinthians 10:5

This is not external discipline, it's internal authority.

You are not at the mercy of your thoughts.

Through Christ, your thoughts are at the mercy of *truth*.

45

Renewal Requires Cooperation with God

God does the renewing —
   but you participate in the process.
   Renewal looks like:

- noticing when your thoughts shift into fear
- asking, "Is this from God?"
- pausing before reacting
- breathing instead of spiraling
- choosing truth over emotion
- redirecting your focus
- returning to Scripture when lies arise
- refusing to rehearse worst-case scenarios

Renewal is restoration with intention.

The Holy Spirit Is Your Helper in Renewal

You are not renewing yourself by willpower.
   The Holy Spirit, the comforter, counselor, and strengthener,
is the One doing the deep work.
   He nudges you when your thoughts drift.
   He whispers when you begin to spiral.
   He reminds you of the truth when lies rise again.
   He comforts you when fear surfaces.
   He aligns your inner world with God's Word.
   You do not renew your mind alone.
   You renew it in partnership with God.

Old Thoughts Don't Disappear — They Get Replaced

You cannot simply "stop thinking" negative thoughts.
   Your mind cannot work from emptiness.
   It needs something *better* to hold onto.
   Renewal happens when you replace:

- fear with faith
- lies with truth
- control with trust
- anxiety with prayer
- overthinking with surrender
- shame with identity
- doubt with Scripture

A renewed mind is not empty, it is filled with the right things.

Renewal Isn't Loud — It's Subtle

Many women expect renewal to feel dramatic.
   But most renewal feels like small shifts:

- you pause instead of panic
- you pray instead of spiral
- you reflect instead of react
- you breathe instead of brace
- you ask God before assuming the worst
- you choose hope when negativity tries to take over

Renewal is quiet, but powerful.
   Invisible at first, but undeniable over time.

47

What a Renewed Mind Feels Like

A renewed mind does not mean a perfect mind.
  It means:

- you are quicker to return to God
- your emotions feel less overwhelming
- your thoughts feel less chaotic
- you recognize lies faster
- you rebound from fear sooner
- you feel anchored instead of tossed
- you experience clarity
- you experience peace
- you experience God in the details

Renewal is the beginning of freedom.

A Truth to Hold Onto

**Renewal doesn't change your life instantly —
  but it changes the way you live your life every day.**

Closing Prayer

Lord, renew my mind in ways I cannot do on my own. Uproot the thoughts that have taken root in fear, shame, or doubt. Plant new thoughts that reflect Your truth, Your peace, and Your presence. Shape my perspective, soften my heart, and transform the way I think. Help me cooperate with Your work in me, trusting that renewal is happening layer by layer. In Jesus' name, amen.

7

Rewrite — Speaking Life Over Yourself

Words have power.

Not just the words spoken out loud, but the words whispered in your mind and rehearsed in your heart.

Many women live in a constant internal dialogue that shapes how they see themselves, how they make decisions, and how they walk through the world.

If your life feels heavy, part of that weight may be the words you speak to yourself day after day, the quiet sentences that others never hear, but God hears clearly.

This chapter is about rewriting those inner words so they reflect the truth God has spoken over you.

Your Inner Voice Shapes Your Reality

Most women do not realize how much influence their inner voice has.

The mind repeats phrases so often that they become beliefs, and beliefs grow into identity.

You may not say these words out loud, but your heart hears

them:

"I am not enough."
"I always get this wrong."
"I mess everything up."
"I should be doing better."
"Everyone else has it together."
"I am too emotional."
"I am too difficult."
"I am not worthy of love."
"I am always a burden."

These are not simple thoughts.
They are stories.
And stories shape your life.

Where Your Inner Words Come From

Your inner language is shaped by:

· childhood experiences
· relationships
· trauma and disappointment
· labels others put on you
· past failures
· culture and environment
· seasons of exhaustion
· spiritual battles
· lies the enemy planted
· fears you never named

These influences create sentences that embed themselves inside you.

Over time, you stop questioning them.

You start believing them.

And eventually, you repeat them without even noticing.

But here is the truth:

You do not have to keep repeating words that God never spoke.

God Has Spoken Better Words Over You

Scripture is filled with identity statements that rewrite your inner language with truth:

Who God Says You Are

You are loved.

"This is love: not that we loved God, but that He loved us…"

1 John 4:10

You are chosen.

"You are a chosen people, a royal priesthood, a holy nation, God's special possession."

1 Peter 2:9

You are enough in Christ.

"Not that we are competent in ourselves… but our competence comes from God."

2 Corinthians 3:5

You are His workmanship.

"For we are God's handiwork, created in Christ Jesus to do good works…"

Ephesians 2:10

You are made new.

"If anyone is in Christ, the new creation has come. The old has gone, the new is here."

2 Corinthians 5:17

You are held.

"Do not fear, for I am with you... I will strengthen you and help you."

Isaiah 41:10

You are valuable.

"You are worth more than many sparrows."

Matthew 10:30–31

You are forgiven.

"If we confess our sins, He is faithful and just to forgive us..."

1 John 1:9

You are strengthened.

"I can do all things through Christ who strengthens me."

Philippians 4:13

You are never alone.

"The Lord your God is with you wherever you go."

Joshua 1:9

God's words build.

God's words restore.

God's words lift.

God's words reshape.

God's words rewrite the broken sentences you have carried for years.

Why Negative Words Stick So Easily

Negative words feel familiar.

Your brain holds onto anything that feels protective, even if it hurts.

For example:

"I should not expect much" feels safer than "God can surprise me."

"I am not good enough" feels safer than "God has equipped me."

"I have to figure this out alone" feels safer than "God will help me."

"Nothing ever works out for me" feels safer than "God is doing a new thing."

Negative words protect you from disappointment.

But they also limit your growth.

And God is not a God of limitation.

He is a God of transformation.

You Cannot Renew Your Mind Without Rewriting Your Words

Renewal begins the moment you confront the sentences that have shaped your thinking.

Ask yourself:

What have I been saying about myself that God never said about me?

What labels have I accepted that do not align with His truth?

What internal phrases have shaped my fears?

What repeated sentences have kept me small?

What words have I allowed to become identity?

Rewriting is not pretending.

Rewriting is replacing.

You replace what is false with what is true.

How to Rewrite Your Words With God's Truth

Here is a simple and powerful practice:

Step One: Identify the sentence you repeat.

Example: "I am not strong enough."

Step Two: Compare it with Scripture.

What does God say about your strength?

Step Three: Write the sentence again through God's truth.

"I can do all things through Christ who strengthens me."

Step Four: Repeat the new sentence until it becomes familiar.

This is how rewriting begins.

Slowly.

Intentionally.

Faithfully.

This Is Not Manifestation, This Is Biblical Identity

Speaking truth over yourself is not manifestation.

It is agreeing with what God already declared.

Words do not create power.

God's truth holds the power, and your words come into agreement with that power.

You are not commanding your future.

You are aligning your heart with God's voice rather than the enemy's.

Rewriting your words is a spiritual practice, not a self centered one.

What Happens When You Rewrite Your Inner Language

When you begin speaking God's truth, even softly, even uncer-tainly, even awkwardly at first, your inner world slowly shifts.

You begin to trust differently

You begin to think differently

You begin to choose differently

You begin to breathe differently

You begin to respond differently

You begin to see yourself through God's eyes rather than your fears

Your inner voice becomes a place of encouragement instead of criticism.

Your thoughts become a safe place instead of a battlefield.

And slowly, a renewed identity is formed.

A Truth to Hold Onto

Your words are either building your faith or feeding your fear. God is inviting you to speak life again.

Closing Prayer

Lord, help me rewrite the words I speak over myself. Show me every sentence that does not reflect Your truth. Replace my inner criticism with confidence in You. Replace my self doubt with Your promises. Fill my mind with the identity You have spoken over me since the beginning. Teach me to agree with Your voice more than my fears. Help me speak life, hope, peace, and truth over my mind and my future. In Jesus' name, amen.

8

Reframe — Seeing Hard Seasons Through God's Eyes

Hard seasons can make your world feel small.

Pain narrows your focus.

Fear clouds your vision.

Waiting stretches your hope thin.

And when you are hurting or confused, it becomes natural to see your life through the lens of what feels wrong, missing, uncertain, or broken.

But the way life looks to you is not always the way life looks to God.

God sees beyond the moment you are standing in.

He sees the purpose behind the pressure.

He sees the healing beneath the hurt.

He sees the growth that is rising beneath the surface.

He sees the future that is forming from the very places that feel painful right now.

Reframing your season is not pretending everything is okay.

Reframing is learning to see what God sees, even when you are walking through the hardest chapters of your story.

Your Perspective Shapes Your Experience

Your perspective is powerful.

It can lift you or weigh you down.

It can open your heart or close it.

It can give you hope or drain it.

Two people can walk through the same situation and experience it completely differently simply because of how they see it.

Pain says, "This is the end."

God says, "This is the turning point."

Fear says, "Something is wrong."

God says, "Something is being refined."

Disappointment says, "You were forgotten."

God says, "I am carefully guiding you."

Your feelings are real.

But they are not always accurate reflections of God's work in your life.

God's Perspective Is Higher Than Yours

You see today.

God sees your entire lifetime.

You see the step in front of you.

God sees the path beneath your feet.

You see the delay.

God sees the timing.

You see the loss.

God sees the restoration.

You see the brokenness.

God sees the rebuilding.

Your perspective is limited, but God's is perfect.

He is not guessing, hoping, or reacting.

He is leading, shaping, and working with clarity that you do not yet have.

Isaiah 55:9 reminds us, *"As the heavens are higher than the earth, so are My ways higher than your ways and My thoughts than your thoughts."*

You may not understand the season you are in, but God understands exactly what He is doing through it.

Hard Seasons Become Holy Ground in God's Hands

Sometimes the most difficult seasons are the ones that carry the greatest blessing.

Not because the pain is good, but because the pain is purposeful.

God never wastes a storm.

He never wastes a waiting season.

He never wastes a heartbreak.

He uses hard seasons to

Strengthen your faith

Deepen your trust

Refine your character

Expose lies you believed

Reveal hidden wounds

Prepare you for the next chapter

Draw you closer to Him

Align you with your purpose

What feels like breaking is often building.

What feels like loss is often leading to growth.

What feels like an ending is often the beginning of something new.

Scripture Shows Us What It Means to Reframe

Joseph's story looked like rejection, betrayal, and loss.

But through God's eyes, every step was preparing him for influence and leadership.

Ruth's story looked like devastation and grief.

Through God's eyes, she was walking into redemption, family, and legacy.

David's years of waiting looked like delay.

Through God's eyes, every hidden season was shaping the heart of a king.

Scripture teaches us that God's plans rarely look logical in the moment, but they always reveal purpose in time.

You Can Ask God for His Perspective

When your heart feels overwhelmed or confused, God invites you to ask Him what He sees.

Pray

"Lord, show me the part of this story that I cannot see."

"Help me understand what You are forming in me."

"Open my eyes to Your purpose in this season."

"Remind me that You are near, even when I do not feel it."

Reframing is not denial.

Reframing is faith in practice.

It is choosing to look for God's fingerprints even when the story feels unfinished.

Reframing Helps You Notice God in the Details

When you begin to reframe your season, you will notice things you once overlooked
    The friend who checks on you
    The strength you gained through discomfort
    The wisdom that came from waiting
    The peace that suddenly feels possible
    The doors God closed that were not meant for you
    The growth that could only come through pressure
    The protection that was hidden in the "no"
    God's presence becomes more visible when you stop focusing only on the pain and begin looking for His purpose.

Reframing Does Not Change the Season, But It Changes You

Reframing does not remove the hurt.
    It anchors you in hope.
    Reframing does not erase your emotions.
    It helps you understand them.
    Reframing does not end the season immediately.
    It strengthens you to walk through it with faith.
    Reframing does not rush the process.
    It helps you trust the One who is guiding it.
    This is where growth begins.
    This is where transformation takes root.
    This is where you begin to see your story with the clarity only God can give.

A Truth to Hold Onto

Your hard season is not a sign that God is absent.
   It is a sign that God is doing a deeper work in you than you can see right now.

Closing Prayer

Lord, help me see my life the way You see it. Where I see confusion, show me clarity. Where I see delay, show me preparation. Where I see loss, show me the seeds of restoration. Lift my perspective so I can recognize Your purpose even in the places that feel painful or uncertain. Teach me to reframe my season according to Your truth, Your presence, and Your faithfulness. In Jesus' name, amen.

9

Rebuild — Becoming the Woman God Designed You to Be

Renewal begins in the mind, but rebuilding happens in the life.

It is the process of becoming, growing, and stepping into the woman God always intended you to be.

Rebuilding is not instant.

It is intentional.

It is patient.

It is sacred.

This chapter invites you to rise from the inside out, one small act of faith at a time, as God strengthens your identity, your confidence, and your purpose.

Rebuilding Begins After Release and Renewal

Once you release what was too heavy, and once God begins renewing your thoughts, you finally create space for Him to rebuild what was broken.

Rebuilding requires three things

A surrendered heart

A renewed mind
A willing spirit
God never forces transformation.
He builds on the space you allow Him to shape.

God Rebuilds You With Care and Precision

You are not a rushed project in God's hands.
You are not being pieced together quickly or carelessly.
You are being rebuilt with intention.
Isaiah 58:12 says, *"You will be called the Repairer of Broken Walls, Restorer of Streets with Dwellings."*
Restore.
Repair.
Rebuild.
These are God's words for you.
He rebuilds you by
Strengthening your identity
Restoring your confidence
Healing emotional wounds
Correcting false beliefs
Developing spiritual maturity
Rebalancing your priorities
Reestablishing your peace
Deepening your trust
Clarifying your calling

Rebuilding Often Looks Small at First

Rebuilding rarely begins with big moments.
  It starts quietly, almost invisibly.
  You choose peace instead of panic.
  You choose prayer instead of fear.
  You choose truth instead of lies.
  You choose boundaries instead of burnout.
  You choose rest instead of pressure.
  You choose surrender instead of control.
  These small choices build a strong, steady foundation.

God Rebuilds What Was Broken by Life

Life may have taken pieces from you, but God is a master builder.
  What you lost is not lost to Him.
  He rebuilds what life tried to tear down.
  Where you were rejected, He rebuilds belonging.
  Where you were discouraged, He rebuilds confidence.
  Where you were weary, He rebuilds strength.
  Where you were overlooked, He rebuilds purpose.
  Where you were wounded, He rebuilds healing.
  Psalm 147:3 reminds us, *"He heals the brokenhearted and binds up their wounds."*
  God does not just heal wounds.
  He rebuilds the whole heart.

You Are Part of the Process

Rebuilding is both divine and practical.
   God rebuilds your spirit.
   You rebuild your habits.
   God restores your identity.
   You walk in confidence.
   God renews your mind.
   You practice new patterns.
   Rebuilding is a partnership where His power meets your participation.

Your Life Begins to Reflect the Work God Is Doing

As God rebuilds you, your life begins to change from the inside out.
   Your relationships shift
   Your boundaries strengthen
   Your peace deepens
   Your choices become healthier
   Your reactions soften
   Your values clarify
   Your confidence grows, not from pride, but from identity
   You become the woman God formed you to be long before fear, loss, or exhaustion tried to rewrite your story.

A Truth to Hold Onto

God is not just repairing you.
   He is remaking you into someone stronger, wiser, and more anchored than before.

Closing Prayer

Lord, rebuild the parts of me that life has worn down. Strengthen my identity, restore my confidence, and heal the places that still feel fragile. Give me the courage to walk in the transformation You are forming within me. Help me partner with You in rebuilding my thoughts, my habits, my relationships, and my purpose. Shape me into the woman You designed me to be, steady, secure, and rooted in You. In Jesus' name, amen.

10

Rise — Stepping Into the Woman God Is Calling You to Be

There comes a moment when the healing God has been doing inside you begins to show on the outside.

Not because everything in your life is suddenly perfect.

Not because all your problems have disappeared.

Not because you feel completely fearless or fully prepared.

You rise because **God has strengthened you from the inside out.**

You rise because **your identity is becoming clearer.**

You rise because **the burden is no longer yours to carry.**

You rise because **you are no longer living by the lies that once shaped you.**

Rising is not loud.

Rising is intentional.

Rising is spiritual maturity taking root.

Rising is the quiet courage to walk in who God says you are, instead of who life tried to convince you to be.

This chapter is an invitation to rise into the woman God created you to become.

Rising Begins When You Believe God's Words Over Your Own Fears

Your fears tell you to stay small.

Your doubts tell you to stay quiet.

Your insecurities tell you to stay hidden.

Your past tells you to stay cautious.

But God tells you something very different.

"Arise, shine, for your light has come, and the glory of the Lord rises upon you."

Isaiah 60:1

God would not call you to rise if He had not already placed His glory within you.

You rise because **He has equipped you.**

You rise because **He has prepared you.**

You rise because **He has spoken purpose over you.**

Rising Is Not About Perfection, It Is About Position

Rising does not mean you never feel anxious.

It means anxiety no longer leads your life.

Rising does not mean you never feel unqualified.

It means you lean on the God who calls the unqualified.

Rising does not mean you never feel uncertain.

It means you choose obedience even when you do not see the entire path.

Rising is not about being perfect.

It is about taking your position as God's daughter.

When You Rise, the Enemy Loses His Grip

The enemy works hardest when you are discouraged, disappointed, or weary.

But once you begin to rise, once you step into the strength God has placed inside you, the lies lose their power.

You rise when you

Choose truth over fear

Choose faith over doubt

Choose obedience over comfort

Choose identity over insecurity

Choose God's voice over the enemy's whisper

Every time you rise, hell loses its hold and heaven strengthens your spirit.

Rising Is an Act of Faithfulness

Sometimes rising looks bold.

Sometimes rising looks quiet.

Sometimes rising looks like taking a new step.

Sometimes rising looks like trying again after a hard season.

Sometimes rising looks like letting God rebuild what you thought was lost.

Rising is not always dramatic.

Often, it is simple.

Often, it is gentle.

Often, it is private.

But it is always holy.

Because rising is you saying,

"Lord, I trust who You are making me."

God Calls You to Rise Even When You Feel Inadequate

Moses did not feel ready.
  Gideon did not feel brave.
  Esther did not feel safe.
  Jeremiah did not feel qualified.
  David did not feel grown enough.
  Yet God still called them to rise.
  Because God does not choose people based on confidence.
  He chooses people based on purpose.
  He is not calling you because you feel strong.
  He is calling you because **He is strong in you.**

Rising Requires Letting Go of the Old Version of Yourself

Rising into the woman God is forming you to be requires releasing the earlier version of yourself.
  The version shaped by fear
  The version shaped by rejection
  The version shaped by insecurity
  The version shaped by survival
  The version shaped by exhaustion
  The version shaped by lies
  You cannot rise while holding onto a version of yourself that God has already healed you from.

This Is What Rising Looks Like in Your Daily Life

Rising is
  Standing firm when fear tries to convince you to retreat
  Speaking kindly to yourself when old criticism resurfaces

71

Choosing rest instead of burnout
Walking away from what hurts your spirit
Believing God has good plans for your future
Setting boundaries that protect your peace
Showing up for your calling even when you feel unprepared
Trusting God's guidance more than your emotions
These choices build the life God intended for you.

You Are Rising Into Strength, Not Striving Toward It

Striving says
   "I need to earn my worth."
   Rising says
   "I am living from the worth God already gave me."
   Striving says
   "I need to prove myself."
   Rising says
   "God has already approved me."
   Striving is exhausting.
   Rising is empowering.
   God is not calling you to strive.
   He is calling you to rise.

A Truth to Hold Onto

You are not rising alone.
   God is rising within you.
   Every step forward is evidence that His strength is becoming your strength.

Closing Prayer

Lord, help me rise into the woman You have created me to be. Strengthen my spirit where fear once lived. Lift my confidence where insecurity once held me back. Guide me as I step into the calling You have placed on my life. Remind me that I rise not by my own power, but by Yours. Continue to grow me, shape me, and lead me into the future You have prepared for me. In Jesus' name, amen.

11

Relationships — Loving Others Without Losing Yourself

Relationships are powerful.

They can strengthen you or drain you.

They can draw you closer to God or pull you away from peace.

They can reflect healing or reveal wounds you have tried to ignore.

For many women, relationships are where the weight of life becomes the heaviest.

You carry emotional responsibility for people you love, you try to fix what is broken, you try to maintain peace at the expense of your own well being, and you stay connected to people who may not be healthy for your heart.

But relationships were never meant to be places where you lose yourself.

They were meant to be places where the love of Christ flows through you and around you, in balance and in truth.

This chapter is an invitation to see relationships in a new way, through the lens of wisdom, boundaries, compassion, and emotional freedom.

Healthy Relationships Begin With a Healthy Mind

Once God begins renewing your thoughts, it becomes much easier to see relationships clearly.

A renewed mind allows you to

Recognize unhealthy patterns

Choose people who value your peace

Respond instead of react

Set boundaries without guilt

Love without losing yourself

Many of the relationship struggles you faced in the past were not because you were unloving.

They were because you were exhausted, drained, or living from old patterns.

A healed mind creates healthier relationships.

Love Does Not Mean Overextending Yourself

Many women confuse love with overfunctioning.

You give too much, forgive too quickly, absorb too many emotions, and stay connected to people who do not honor your heart.

But Scripture does not require you to lose yourself to love others.

"Love your neighbor as yourself."

–Mark 12:31

This means you were supposed to love yourself too.

Love is not self abandonment.

Love is not allowing others to treat you carelessly.

Love is not silence when your heart is hurting.

75

Love is patient and kind, not exhausting and depleting.
Love protects, it does not destroy.
Love builds, it does not drain.

Boundaries Are Biblical, Not Harsh

Boundaries are not a sign of weakness or selfishness.
Boundaries are wisdom.
Jesus had boundaries.
He withdrew from crowds to rest.
He said no.
He protected His peace.
He spent time with people who were aligned with His purpose.
He walked away from hostility when necessary.
A boundary is simply saying,
"This is where I end and where someone else's responsibility begins."
Boundaries protect your emotional, spiritual, and mental health.
They are not walls used to keep people out.
They are doors used to let the right people in.

You Cannot Heal People by Carrying Their Burdens for Them

It is natural to want to help.
It is natural to want to support people who are hurting.
But you cannot be the solution to someone else's pain.
You cannot save someone who is not ready to change.
You cannot force healing that can only come from God.
Galatians 6:5 says,

"Each one should carry their own load."
You can love others.
You can pray for them.
You can encourage them.
But you cannot live their healing journey for them.
You are responsible for kindness, not rescue.
You are responsible for compassion, not control.
You are responsible for grace, not self sacrifice that destroys your peace.

Not Every Relationship Is Meant to Continue

Rebuilding your life may require releasing relationships that are unhealthy or harmful.
Painful but honest truth
Some people cannot stay in the next chapter of your story.
Some relationships were seasonal.
Some connections taught you what you needed to know.
Some goodbyes were protection.
Some distance was God's direction.
You are not being unloving by letting go.
You are making space for healthier, holier relationships that reflect your growth.

God Will Send People Who Strengthen Your Spirit

As God heals and renews you, He will surround you with people who
Encourage your growth
Respect your boundaries
Value your peace

Speak life into you
Pray with you and for you
Support your purpose
Bring clarity instead of confusion
Add emotional safety
Reflect God's love
These are covenant friendships.
These are divine connections.
These are the people who walk with you in faith and truth.
Pray for these relationships.
God knows exactly who belongs in your life.

Healing Your Heart Helps Heal Your Relationships

Once you heal the inner parts of your heart, you will notice three things happening in your relationships:

1. You respond from wisdom instead of wounds.

Your emotional patterns shift because your heart is no longer reacting from old hurt.

2. You choose peace instead of chaos.

You no longer tolerate what drains you.

3. You stop accepting love that requires you to shrink yourself.

You begin choosing relationships that match your healing.

Your external relationships begin to reflect your internal transformation.

A Truth to Hold Onto

Healthy love does not require you to lose yourself.
  God will teach you how to love others and protect your heart at the same time.

Closing Prayer

Lord, guide me in my relationships. Give me the wisdom to see what is healthy and what is harmful. Strengthen me where I need boundaries, restore me where I have been hurt, and surround me with people who reflect Your love and truth. Help me love others with grace without losing myself in the process. Teach me to walk in relationships that honor You and protect the peace You are building within me. In Jesus' name, amen.

12

Surrender – Living With Peace, Trust, and Confidence in God

Surrender is not a moment.

Surrender is a lifestyle.

It is a daily choosing, a daily trusting, a daily releasing of what was never meant to be carried alone.

You spent years surviving.

You spent years holding on.

You spent years building strength through fear instead of faith.

But now, God is inviting you to live in a different rhythm — a rhythm shaped by peace, guided by trust, and filled with His presence.

This chapter is the heart of your journey.

It is where everything you have released, renewed, reframed, and rebuilt becomes a way of life, not just a passing moment of clarity.

Surrender Is Trust in Its Purest Form

Surrender is not weakness.

Surrender is not defeat.

Surrender is not losing control.

Surrender is trusting God more than you trust yourself.

It is trusting His timing more than your own.

It is trusting His wisdom more than your emotions.

It is trusting His plan more than your expectations.

Proverbs 3:5 reminds us,

"Trust in the Lord with all your heart and lean not on your own understanding."

Your understanding is limited.

His understanding is limitless.

Surrender happens the moment you stop leaning on your own strength and begin leaning fully into Him.

You Surrender When You Let God Be God

You cannot control everything.

You cannot fix everyone.

You cannot predict the future.

You cannot carry burdens alone.

You cannot heal wounds that only God can reach.

Surrender is you saying

"God, this belongs to You.

I trust You.

I release my grip."

And the beautiful thing about God is this

He receives what you surrender with gentleness.

He carries what you place in His hands with perfect care.

He never asks you to release something that He will not redeem.

Surrender Looks Like Peaceful Obedience

Surrendered living is not passive.

It does not mean sitting still and hoping things magically improve.

Surrender is active trust.

Surrender looks like

Obeying when God nudges your heart

Letting go when He closes a door

Resting when He says be still

Stepping forward when He says move

Choosing faith when fear rises

Praying instead of panicking

Being still enough to hear His voice

Surrender is a posture.

A position.

A heart that says

"God, whatever You ask, I am willing."

Surrender Brings a Peace That Cannot Be Manufactured

You cannot force peace.

You cannot fake peace.

You cannot create peace while still clinging to burdens.

Peace comes when your hands release what your heart was never created to hold.

Philippians 4:7 promises,

"The peace of God, which transcends all understanding, will

guard your hearts and your minds in Christ Jesus."

This peace is not emotional numbness.

This peace is not the absence of problems.

This peace is the presence of God standing guard over your mind.

Surrender opens the door for that peace to enter.

Surrender Brings You Back Into Alignment

When you stop carrying what is not yours

When you stop forcing what is not God's timing

When you stop holding onto what is hurting you

When you stop fighting battles that are not yours to fight

Your heart realigns.

Your mind resets.

Your spirit rests.

Your steps become steadier because you are walking in rhythm with God.

You begin to see your life through the lens of His faithfulness instead of your fears.

Surrender Helps You Live From Identity Instead of Insecurity

When you surrender, you stop striving for approval.

You stop chasing worth in the wrong places.

You stop measuring yourself by the opinions of people who cannot see what God sees in you.

Surrender anchors you in the truth

You are loved.

You are known.

You are held.
You are chosen.
You are safe in God's hands.
Identity becomes your foundation.
Insecurity loses its voice.

A Surrendered Life Is a Connected Life

Surrender connects you to God in a way striving never could.
   You no longer feel like you are carrying life alone.
   You sense His presence more.
   You hear His voice more clearly.
   You trust His leading more deeply.
   You walk with confidence because your confidence is in Him,
not in yourself.
   A surrendered life is a spiritually connected life.

Surrender Is Not the End of Your Journey. It Is the Beginning.

Surrender positions you to receive
   God's direction
   God's peace
   God's strength
   God's provision
   God's protection
   God's purpose
   Surrender is where God finally has room to move.
   Room to guide.
   Room to heal.
   Room to bless.

Room to build the life He always planned for you.

This is not the end of your story.

This is the beginning of your awakened, aligned, confident life with God.

A Truth to Hold Onto

Surrender is not losing control.

Surrender is placing your life in the hands of a God who has never lost a battle.

Closing Prayer

Lord, teach me to live surrendered. Help me release every burden that was never mine to carry. Calm my fears, steady my heart, and strengthen my trust. Lead me in Your timing, Your wisdom, and Your will. Let my life reflect Your peace and confidence. I place everything in Your hands, knowing You are faithful and good. In Jesus' name, amen.

13

Remember – Holding On to What God Has Done

Spiritual growth is not only about what God is doing right now.

It is also about remembering what God has already done.

When life becomes overwhelming, your mind can quickly forget the victories God brought you through. Your heart can forget the peace He restored. Your spirit can forget the moments He carried you when you had no strength of your own.

But remembrance is powerful.

Remembrance strengthens faith.

Remembrance rebuilds confidence.

Remembrance restores perspective.

Remembrance reminds you who God has always been.

This chapter helps you hold on to the truth that God's faithfulness did not start today.

It has always been with you.

God Repeatedly Tells His People to Remember

All throughout Scripture, God commands His people to remember what He has done.

Deuteronomy 7:18 says,

"Do not be afraid... remember well what the Lord your God did."

Psalm 77:11 says,

"I will remember the deeds of the Lord; yes, I will remember Your miracles of long ago."

Why?

Because forgetfulness leads to fear.

But remembrance leads to faith.

When you remember

the valleys He walked you through

the storms He calmed

the prayers He answered

the peace He restored

the strength He gave

the doors He opened

the protection He provided

the healing He brought

Your heart becomes anchored again.

Your Memory Is a Weapon Against the Enemy

When the enemy whispers

"You're alone,"

you remember

God was with me then, and He is with me now.

When the enemy says

"This is the end,"
you remember
God has brought me through every season before.
When the enemy says
"You cannot handle this,"
you remember
God strengthened me when I was at my weakest.
Your memories of God's faithfulness are not sentimental.
They are spiritual weapons.

Remembering Builds Confidence in God's Future Plans

You may not know what your future holds, but you know the God who holds your future.

Every time you remember what He has done, your heart becomes more confident in what He will do.

You may not see the next step
but you remember that God guided you before.
You may not feel strong enough
but you remember that His strength carried you.
You may not understand this season
but you remember that He worked all things together for good before.

Remembrance is a bridge between your past faith and your future hope.

Create a Personal Record of God's Faithfulness

You can strengthen your spirit by writing down the moments that reflect God's presence in your life.

Write down;

your answered prayers
your unexpected blessings
your protected moments
your breakthroughs
your small victories
your moments of peace
your transformed thoughts
As you write, your spirit will testify

"God has been with me every step."

Your record becomes a testament that God has never left your side.

A Truth to Hold Onto

The God who carried you before will carry you again.
Your memories of His faithfulness are proof that He will not fail you now.

Closing Prayer

Lord, help me remember the moments where Your faithfulness carried me. Bring to mind every answered prayer, every restored peace, every blessing I once overlooked. Strengthen my confidence with the memories of what You have done in my life. Let remembrance become the anchor that keeps me steady when life feels uncertain. In Jesus' name, amen.

14

Reclaim – Taking Back What the Enemy Tried to Steal

There comes a time in every woman's journey when she stops simply healing from what happened and begins reclaiming what was lost.

Reclaiming your confidence.

Reclaiming your joy.

Reclaiming your voice.

Reclaiming your identity.

Reclaiming your peace.

Reclaiming your purpose.

Reclaiming your authority in Christ.

The enemy has taken enough from you.

This chapter is your declaration that you are stepping into everything that belongs to you as a daughter of God.

Reclaiming Begins With Knowing What Is Yours

The enemy cannot take what you do not recognize.

But once you know what belongs to you, you begin to stand with holy boldness.

Your peace is yours.

John 14:27

Your authority is yours.

Luke 10:19

Your identity in Christ is yours.

2 Corinthians 5:17

Your joy is yours.

Psalm 51:12

Your sound mind is yours.

2 Timothy 1:7

Your purpose is yours.

Ephesians 2:10

You are not fighting for victory.

You are fighting from victory.

Jesus already secured what belongs to you.

Reclaiming Means You Stop Agreeing With the Enemy's Lies

For years, the enemy tried to convince you that you were
   not enough
   unworthy
   weak
   unlovable
   broken beyond repair
   forgotten

disqualified

But God says

You are chosen.

You are loved.

You are renewed.

You are restored.

You are strengthened.

You are seen.

You are called.

Reclaiming begins the moment you stop agreeing with lies and start agreeing with God.

Reclaiming Requires Stepping Into Your Identity, Not Shrinking From It

There is nothing holy about shrinking.

There is nothing godly about minimizing yourself.

There is nothing humble about denying the gifts God placed within you.

Reclaiming your identity means you finally stand tall in the truth

I am who God says I am.

I carry what God gave me.

I walk in the authority God placed on my life.

This is not pride.

This is alignment.

Reclaiming Is Spiritual Warfare in Disguise

Every time you reclaim something the enemy tried to destroy, you are fighting in the spirit.

When you choose joy
you reclaim what sorrow tried to steal.
When you choose peace
you reclaim what anxiety tried to suffocate.
When you speak truth
you reclaim what lies tried to distort.
When you set boundaries
you reclaim your emotional safety.
When you walk confidently
you reclaim ground the enemy thought he owned.
Reclaiming is powerful.
Reclaiming is holy.
Reclaiming is warfare.

God Will Restore Everything You Lost in the Process

God is a God of restoration.
He does not return things the same way they left.
He returns them better.

Joel 2:25 says,
"I will restore to you the years the locusts have eaten."
Years of pain.
Years of exhaustion.
Years of fear.
Years of surviving.
None of it is wasted.

God restores time, strength, joy, and hope.
Nothing lost is lost to Him.

A Truth to Hold Onto

This is the season where you reclaim what was taken.
You rise in identity, walk in authority, and live in the freedom Christ paid for.

Closing Prayer

Lord, help me reclaim every part of my life that the enemy tried to steal. Restore my joy, strengthen my voice, renew my confidence, and awaken my purpose. Remind me of the authority You have given me as Your daughter. Lead me into a life of boldness, peace, and freedom. I receive everything You have for me, and I release everything that once held me back. In Jesus' name, amen.

15

Rise Again – Walking in Renewal Every Single Day

Transformation is not a single moment.

Transformation is a rhythm, rising, renewing, surrendering, trusting, again and again as life unfolds.

There will be days when you feel strong and steady.

There will be days when you feel weary and uncertain.

There will be days when you walk boldly in the truth you have learned.

There will be days when old patterns try to pull you backward.

This does not mean you have failed.

It means you are human.

It means you are growing.

It means you are walking with God through a living relationship, not a one-time breakthrough.

The beauty of this journey is not in rising once.

The beauty is that you now know **you can rise again.**

You Are Not the Woman You Once Were

Even if you feel weak on some days, remember this truth

You are not who you were when you started this journey.

You are more aware.

You are more grounded.

You are more surrendered.

You are more discerning.

You are more connected to God's voice.

You are more anchored in truth.

Old fears may whisper, but they no longer define you.

Old wounds may ache, but they no longer control you.

Old lies may surface, but they no longer silence you.

You have changed from the inside out.

Even on your hardest days, you walk with a renewed spirit.

Rising Again Requires Returning to What You Know Is True

When life feels heavy, you rise again by returning to the foundations you've built.

Return to surrender.

Lay everything back at His feet.

Return to Scripture.

Let God's voice rewrite the noise.

Return to truth.

Speak what God says about you, not what fear says about you.

Return to peace.

Slow down. Breathe. Rest in Him again.

Return to boundaries.

Protect what God has restored within you.

Return to remembrance.

Recall the faithfulness that carried you this far.
You rise again not by trying harder, but by returning sooner.

Every Time You Rise Again, You Become Stronger

Each rise builds spiritual muscle.
Each rise strengthens your faith.
Each rise deepens your trust in God.
Each rise reinforces your identity.
Each rise reminds the enemy that he no longer has authority over your mind.
Rising again is not starting over.
Rising again is continuing forward with new wisdom.

God Does Not Expect Perfection. He Invites Persistence.

God is not looking for flawless women.
He is looking for the surrendered ones.
Women who get back up.
Women who call on Him in weakness.
Women who lean on Him when they feel uncertain.
Women who rise again with His strength, not their own.

Proverbs 24:16 reminds us,
"Though the righteous fall seven times, they rise again."
Falling does not disqualify you.
Stumbling does not undo your progress.
Weakness does not disappoint God.
Rising again honors Him.

You Rise Again Because God Is Still Writing Your Story

Your story did not end in the hard place where God began healing you.

Your story did not end in the season you survived.

Your story is still unfolding, beautifully, intentionally, divinely.

There is more purpose.

There is more healing.

There is more growth.

There is more joy.

There is more calling.

There is more restoration.

God is not done with you.

Every chapter of your journey is preparing you for the next.

You rise again because **He is not finished.**

A Truth to Hold Onto

You will rise again, not because you are strong, but because God is faithful.

He lifts you, carries you, strengthens you, and leads you — every single day.

Closing Prayer

Lord, help me rise again each day with Your strength. Remind me that I do not walk alone and that Your presence goes before me and surrounds me. When I feel weak, lift me. When I feel discouraged, speak truth to my heart. When old lies resurface, silence them with

Your voice. Help me walk in the identity, peace, and purpose You have given me. Thank You for the grace that allows me to rise again and again. In Jesus' name, amen.

16

Restore – Healing the Parts No One Sees

Healing does not begin in the places others notice.

Healing begins in the hidden places — the quiet corners of your heart where pain has lived without a name.

There are wounds you learned to function with.

There are fears you learned to numb.

There are disappointments you learned to bury.

There are thoughts you learned to hide.

There are memories you tried to outrun.

But God sees every hidden place, and He is gentle with the parts of you that still ache.

You do not have to pretend you are unhurt to be worthy of healing.

God restores what you are willing to bring into His light.

Restoration Begins With Permission

God does not force restoration.

He invites it.

You must give Him permission to touch the places you have protected, avoided, or ignored.

"He heals the brokenhearted and binds up their wounds."

Psalm 147:3

Some wounds are obvious.

Some wounds are buried.

Some wounds are old.

Some wounds have shaped the way you think, love, fear, and protect yourself.

But every wound is known to God.

And every wound can be restored.

Hidden Pain Shapes Your Life More Than You Realize

Unhealed hurts never stay quiet.

They speak through your reactions.

They shape your relationships.

They influence your thoughts.

They fuel your fears.

They cloud your perspective.

They rewrite your identity.

Restoration is not optional for a renewed mind, it is essential.

You cannot rise fully if pieces of your heart are still held hostage by old wounds.

God Restores You Through Truth, Not Shame

Healing does not come through blame.
   Healing does not come through self-hatred.
   Healing does not come through perfectionism.
   Healing comes through truth.
   Truth reveals what hurt you.
   Truth exposes what shaped you.
   Truth uncovers what the enemy used against you.
   Truth invites God to restore what life took from you.
   Shame hides.
   Truth heals.
   John 8:32 reminds us,
   "You will know the truth, and the truth will set you free."
   God lovingly reveals truth to set you free, not to condemn you.

Restoration Happens Layer by Layer

Healing is not instant.
   Healing is a layering process.
   You may heal one part of your heart, only to discover God is ready to restore another.
   You may forgive one situation, only to realize there is another memory that needs His touch.
   You may release one lie, only to uncover another that shaped your identity.
   But this is not failure.
   This is progress.
   Every layer restored brings more peace.
   Every layer healed brings more clarity.

Every layer released brings more freedom.

God Restores by Touching the Exact Place of Pain

The woman with the issue of blood was not healed by touching Jesus' robe.

Jesus restored her by touching the exact place she hid — her shame and isolation.

He asked, *"Who touched Me?"*

Not because He didn't know.

But because He knew she needed to be seen to be restored.

Your restoration works the same way.

God touches

the memory

the betrayal

the disappointment

the abandonment

the fear

the moment your confidence broke

the moment your heart was wounded

Restoration happens when He meets you in the exact place where the pain began.

Restoration Changes How You See Yourself

When God restores you, you begin to see yourself clearly again.

You stop seeing yourself through past wounds.

You stop defining yourself by what hurt you.

You stop shrinking from memories that once controlled you.

You stop carrying emotional weight that was never yours.

Restoration is God giving you back the pieces of yourself

the enemy tried to steal.

A Truth to Hold Onto

God does not just heal what happened.
   He restores who you were before it happened.

Closing Prayer

Lord, restore the hidden places of my heart. Heal the wounds I have carried silently. Touch the parts of me that still hurt and bring Your peace into the places I have avoided. Remove every lie, every fear, and every memory that has shaped me in ways You never intended. Restore my joy, my confidence, and my identity. Make me whole again in Your presence. In Jesus' name, amen.

17

Rebalance – Building a Life That Protects Your Peace

Life does not automatically create balance.

Life pulls, stretches, demands, and distracts.

Life fills your calendar faster than it fills your spirit.

Life can feel like a constant tug-of-war between what you need, what others expect, and what God is calling you toward.

Rebalancing your life is not about doing more.

Rebalancing is about **aligning your life with what God values**, not what the world pressures you into.

This chapter helps you reclaim your time, restore your margins, and rebuild your rhythms so your life reflects peace instead of pressure.

Balance Begins With Awareness, Not Activity

You cannot change what you do not acknowledge.

And many women live unbalanced, not because they want to, but because they have not stopped long enough to recognize the weight they are carrying.

Balance begins when you honestly ask yourself

What is draining me?

What is distracting me?

What is overwhelming me?

What is no longer serving my spirit?

What am I doing out of guilt instead of purpose?

What am I doing out of fear instead of calling?

Awareness becomes the foundation God uses to rebuild your daily life.

God Never Designed You to Live Overextended

Being busy is not the same as being purposeful.

Being needed is not the same as being called.

Being productive is not the same as being spiritually aligned.

Jesus was never in a hurry.

Never rushed.

Never reactive.

Never frantic.

He moved with purpose.

He rested intentionally.

He withdrew when needed.

He said no.

He protected His peace so He could fulfill His purpose.

If Jesus, the Savior of the world, lived with margin, you are allowed to live with margin too.

Matthew 11:28 reminds us,

"Come to Me, all you who are weary and burdened, and I will give you rest."

Peace is a promise, not a reward for exhaustion.

Rebalancing Requires You to Release What God Didn't Assign

There are things you are carrying that God did not ask you to carry.

Roles

Responsibilities

Relationships

Expectations

Pressures

Commitments

Some of them were seasonal.

Some of them were emotional.

Some of them were rooted in guilt.

Some of them were never meant for you in the first place.

Rebalancing does not always mean doing less.

Sometimes it means doing **only what God assigned**.

Everything else becomes noise.

Peace Grows When You Protect Your Capacity

You have emotional capacity.

Mental capacity.

Spiritual capacity.

Relational capacity.

And everything you say yes to takes space from something else.

Rebalance begins with creating space for what nourishes your spirit.

You protect your peace by

Saying no without guilt

Pausing when life feels rushed
Taking breaks without apologizing
Creating boundaries around your time
Resting before you collapse
Recognizing when you are at capacity

Peace is not a feeling you wait for; peace is a boundary you build.

Your Life Shifts When You Start Living Deliberately

Balanced living is intentional living.

It looks like

Waking up with purpose

Slowing down enough to hear God's voice

Protecting time for rest

Being present instead of distracted

Choosing meaningful relationships

Releasing what drains you

Making space for joy

Listening to your spirit, not your stress

Walking in God's rhythm, not the world's rush

When you live deliberately, balance becomes natural—not forced.

Rebalancing Helps You Experience God More Clearly

When your life is cluttered, God's voice becomes harder to hear.

But when you create margin:

Your spirit becomes quieter

Your thoughts become clearer

Your decisions become wiser

Your emotions become steadier
Your heart becomes more sensitive to God's nudges
Balance is not about time management; balance is about **spiritual clarity**.

A Truth to Hold Onto

You cannot live in peace if your life is built around pressure. Rebalance your days, and your spirit will breathe again.

Closing Prayer

Lord, help me rebalance my life in a way that honors You. Show me what to release, what to protect, and what to prioritize. Teach me to live with margin, peace, and purpose. Quiet the noise that distracts me, and give me the wisdom to build a life that reflects Your rhythm, not the pressure of the world. In Jesus' name, amen.

18

Rooted – Staying Connected to God Daily

Lasting transformation does not come from a single breakthrough.

It comes from daily connection, roots that grow deeper over time, anchoring you in

God's presence, God's truth, and God's peace.

When your roots are shallow, life feels unstable.

Small storms shake you.

Minor stress overwhelms you.

Old patterns resurface quickly.

Fear returns easily.

But when your roots grow deep in God, everything changes.

You become grounded in truth.

You stand steady under pressure.

You hear God's voice more clearly.

You feel His peace more consistently.

You rise with confidence because you are connected to the One who strengthens you.

This chapter is about building a daily, living relationship with God — one that sustains you long after the emotional moment has passed.

Being Rooted Means Staying Close to the Source

You cannot grow without connection.

You cannot flourish without nourishment.

You cannot walk in purpose without remaining close to the One who gives it.

John 15:5 says,

"I am the vine; you are the branches. If you remain in Me and I in you, you will bear much fruit."

Remaining in Him is the key.

Not striving.

Not performing.

Not hustling for holiness.

Simply remaining.

Simply staying connected.

Your strength comes from your Source.

You Stay Rooted Through Daily Surrender

Surrender is not occasional.

Surrender is daily.

You stay rooted when you

give Him your worries each morning

place your decisions in His hands

invite Him into your day

surrender your plans

surrender your reactions

surrender your emotions
surrender your pacing
This does not mean you are weak.
It means you trust the One who sees what you cannot see.
Daily surrender strengthens your roots.

You Stay Rooted Through God's Word

Scripture is not just information; it is nourishment.

It steadies your mind, redirects your focus, and anchors your heart.

When you feel anxious, Scripture becomes your calm.

When you feel uncertain, Scripture becomes your clarity.

When you feel discouraged, Scripture becomes your confidence.

When you feel spiritually dry, Scripture becomes your water.

Psalm 1:2–3 describes you as

"a tree planted by streams of water, which yields its fruit in season and whose leaf does not wither."

Trees planted by water do not panic when the heat comes.

Their roots are deep.

They are nourished.

They are anchored.

You stay rooted in the same way.

You Stay Rooted Through Prayer

Prayer is not a performance.

Prayer is relationship.

Prayer is conversation.

Prayer is connection.

You do not need long, poetic words.
Your prayers can be simple.
"Lord, be with me today."
"Give me strength."
"Show me what I need to see."
"Help me respond with grace."
"I trust You with this."
Prayer does not change God.
Prayer changes you.
It softens your heart, aligns your spirit, and clears your mind.
Prayer keeps you rooted.

You Stay Rooted Through Quiet Moments With God

Your soul needs stillness.
Your mind needs silence.
Your spirit needs rest.
Spending quiet moments with God gives your heart room to breathe.
It creates space for His voice to rise above the noise.
Even five minutes of stillness can reset your entire day.
You stay rooted when you choose
presence over pressure
quiet over chaos
connection over distraction
Your peace grows in the stillness.

When You Stay Rooted, Your Life Bears Fruit

Being rooted is not only about survival.
  It is about fruit — visible evidence of God's work in your life.
  When you are rooted, people will notice
  your peace
  your joy
  your steadiness
  your wisdom
  your strength
  your compassion
  your patience
  your clarity
  your confidence
  This fruit is not forced.
  It grows naturally from deep connection with God.
  You were created to flourish.

A Truth to Hold Onto

Staying rooted does not require perfection; it requires connection.
  God grows what He is connected to.

Closing Prayer

Lord, help me stay rooted in You. Draw my heart into a deeper connection with Your presence. Teach me to remain, to trust, and to rest in Your strength. Nourish my spirit through Your Word, calm my mind through prayer, and anchor my heart in Your truth. Let my life bear fruit that reflects Your goodness. Keep me close, steady, and grounded in You every day. In Jesus' name, amen.

19

Renewed Habits – Living Out Your Transformation

Transformation is not just a moment with God.

Transformation becomes real when it shapes the way you live each day.

Renewed habits are the daily choices that support the healing, the clarity, and the peace God is cultivating in your life. They turn spiritual growth into a spiritual lifestyle. They take the truth you've learned and weave it into your routine.

Your life changes when your habits change.

Your mind grows healthier when your patterns align with truth.

Your heart feels lighter when your daily choices protect your peace.

Your days become sacred ground when your habits honor God.

This chapter will guide you through building the habits that anchor your transformation.

You Don't Rise by Motivation, You Rise by Habit

Motivation is emotional.
It comes and goes.
It rises and falls.
It is strong one morning and silent the next.
Habits are different.
Habits carry you when motivation fades.
Habits reinforce what God has done in your spirit.
Habits make consistency possible.
Habits take the pressure off your emotions.
Habits build the life you want, one day at a time.
Your renewed mind deserves renewed patterns.

God Desires Consistency, Not Perfection

Perfection is not the goal of spiritual habits.
Connection is.
Consistency is.
Obedience is.
Lamentations 3:23 reminds us,
"His mercies are new every morning."
Every morning is a reset.
Every morning is a fresh start.
Every morning God invites you to begin again.
Renewed habits are built not by flawless days, but by faithful ones.

Habit One: Begin Your Day With God

When you begin your morning with God, the entire tone of your day shifts.

It does not have to be long or complicated.

It can be simple:

A short prayer

A Scripture verse

A quiet breath

A whispered "Lord, be with me"

A moment of gratitude

A few minutes in the Word

This small practice anchors your thoughts, calms your spirit, and reminds your heart of who is leading your day.

How you start your morning shapes your mindset for everything that follows.

Habit Two: Speak Truth Over Yourself Daily

Your mind needs truth the way your body needs nourishment.

Speak truth aloud.

Declare who God says you are.

Break agreement with old lies.

Rewrite your thoughts with Scripture.

Even one minute of truth can override an entire day of fear.

Truth spoken consistently becomes belief.

Belief becomes identity.

Identity becomes transformation.

Habit Three: Protect Your Peace With Boundaries

Boundaries are not occasional decisions.
   They are daily habits that protect the work God is doing in your life.
   You protect your peace by
   Saying no when needed
   Resting when your spirit feels overwhelmed
   Limiting chaotic environments
   Monitoring what you allow into your mind
   Creating emotional and relational safeguards
   Listening to your body and mind
   Boundaries are habits that keep your spirit healthy.

Habit Four: Practice Gratitude Every Day

Gratitude is a spiritual weapon.
   It shifts your mindset from lack to abundance.
   It trains your heart to see God in the details.
   It softens discouragement.
   It reshapes your perspective.
   A simple daily gratitude practice can transform your emotional atmosphere.
   Write three things each day
   small or big, simple or meaningful
   that reflect God's goodness.
   Gratitude builds joy — and joy strengthens your spirit.

Habit Five: Create Rhythms of Rest

Rest is not laziness.
  Rest is respect for the limits God created in you.
  You honor God by caring for your mind and body.
  Daily rest
  Evening wind down
  Sabbath moments
  Quiet time without screens
  Creating margin in your schedule
  These rhythms keep your mind clear, your emotions steady, and your heart open to God's presence.
  Rest is a holy habit.

Habit Six: Stay Rooted in Community

Isolation weakens you.
  Community strengthens you.
  God designed you to be supported, uplifted, encouraged, and prayed for by others.
  Community helps you
  Stay accountable
  Feel connected
  Grow spiritually
  Stay encouraged during storms
  Develop healthy relationships
  Walk in unity and purpose
  Connection is a spiritual habit that nourishes your soul.

Your Habits Are an Act of Faith

Renewed habits say
  "I believe God is changing me."
  "I am committed to living differently."
  "I am building a life that reflects healing."
  "I am aligning my daily choices with who God says I am."
  Your habits are evidence of your transformation.

A Truth to Hold Onto

Your life changes when your habits change.
  Renewed habits create room for God's work to take root in your daily life.

Closing Prayer

Lord, help me build habits that honor You. Strengthen my desire to stay connected to Your presence each day. Guide my thoughts, my routines, my boundaries, and my choices. Teach me to create patterns that support the healing and transformation You've started within me. Let my daily habits become a reflection of Your love, wisdom, and peace. In Jesus' name, amen.

20

Resilience – Standing Strong When Life Shifts Again

Healing does not guarantee that life will never shake again.

Growth does not mean challenges will never return.

Even with a renewed mind and a surrendered heart, you will still face moments of stress, hurt, uncertainty, and unexpected storms.

But the difference now is this

You are no longer the woman who breaks easily.

You are the woman who rises with resilience.

Resilience is not the absence of struggle.

Resilience is the ability to stand firm when the struggle comes.

It is the strength to bend without breaking, the faith to trust without seeing, and the confidence to endure without losing who you are in Christ.

This chapter teaches you how to keep standing strong when life shifts again.

True Resilience Is Rooted in God, Not in Self-Strength

The world teaches women to "push through," "toughen up," and "handle everything on your own."

But biblical resilience looks very different.
It says
"When I am weak, then I am strong."
2 Corinthians 12:10
It says
"God is my refuge and strength."
Psalm 46:1
It says
"The Lord is the strength of my life."
Psalm 27:1
Resilience does not come from self-reliance.
Resilience comes from God-reliance.
He becomes your strength when your strength ends.

You Are Stronger Than You Were Before

Everything you have walked through, every chapter in this book, every step in your healing, has strengthened you in ways you cannot always see.
You are more grounded.
You are more discerning.
You are more surrendered.
You are more emotionally aware.
You are more spiritually mature.
You are more connected to God's voice.
You are more confident in who you are and whose you are.

Your resilience is not accidental.

It was formed in every moment you trusted God instead of fear.

You Will Face Hard Days, But You Will Not Face Them Alone

God never promised an easy life.

He promised a present one.

Isaiah 43:2 says,

"When you pass through the waters, I will be with you."

Not if you pass through the waters

When.

Not if you walk through the fire

When.

But the promise is greater than the trial

"I will be with you."

Resilience grows when you remember that God walks with you through every shift, every storm, every unknown.

Resilience Is Built Through What You've Survived

Nothing you've been through is wasted.

Not the heartbreak.

Not the pressure.

Not the anxiety.

Not the betrayal.

Not the disappointment.

Not the season that nearly broke you.

Every storm strengthened something in you.

Every wilderness taught you something about God.

Every setback built spiritual muscle.

Every tear watered seeds of resilience.

Your resilience is the harvest of everything you have already overcome.

Resilience Means You Bounce Back Faster

You may still feel fear, but you no longer live in it.

You may still feel overwhelmed, but you no longer collapse beneath it.

You may still feel uncertain, but you no longer spiral from it.

You may still feel discouraged, but you no longer stay stuck in it.

Resilience does not remove emotion.

Resilience gives emotion a place to rest, in God's hands instead of your own.

Resilience says

"I may bend today, but I will not break."

"I may fall, but I will rise again."

"I may not know what is coming, but I know God is with me."

Resilience Is a Result of Renewed Thinking

When your mind is healthy, your spirit becomes steady.

You stand strong because

You speak truth instead of repeating lies

You recognize patterns instead of falling into them

You choose peace instead of panic

You lean into Scripture instead of fear

You surrender your expectations instead of forcing outcomes

The renewed mind you have built throughout this book is the

foundation of your resilience.

Resilience Becomes Your Testimony

People will notice it.
   People will feel it.
   People will see God's hand on you.
   Your stability becomes a witness.
   Your peace becomes a testimony.
   Your strength becomes a reflection of God's faithfulness.
   Your endurance becomes an overflow of His presence.
   Your life will preach louder than your words.

A Truth to Hold Onto

You are resilient not because life is easy, but because God is steady.
   Nothing you face can shake what God has strengthened within you.

Closing Prayer

Lord, make me resilient. Strengthen the parts of me that still feel fragile. Remind me that I never face battles alone. Build within me a faith that stands firm, a peace that remains steady, and a confidence that withstands every shift in life. Thank You for being my refuge, my strength, and my constant source of resilience. Help me rise again and again through Your power. In Jesus' name, amen.

21

Radiate – Becoming a Light to Others

Healing never stops with you.

What God does within you naturally begins to flow through you, into your home, your friendships, your work, your family, and every space your feet touch.

When God renews your mind, restores your heart, and rebuilds your identity, you begin to **radiate** something different.

Your presence shifts atmospheres.

Your peace calms others.

Your strength encourages the weary.

Your faith inspires the discouraged.

Your transformation becomes a testimony without you having to say a single word.

This chapter is about stepping into the influence God has already placed within you.

You Radiate What God Has Rebuilt in You

Before healing, you radiated survival.
You radiated exhaustion.
You radiated worry.
You radiated self-protection.
You radiated fear.
But now, God has given you something new to carry.
When God restores your heart, He restores your radiance.
You begin to radiate
peace in chaotic spaces
strength in fragile moments
wisdom where confusion once lived
joy that rises despite circumstance
faith that steadies those around you
A healed woman becomes a light in dark places.

You Don't Have to Try to Shine — Light Happens Naturally

Jesus said,
"You are the light of the world."
Matthew 5:14
He did not say,
"You must become the light."
"You need to earn the light."
"You should pretend to be the light."
He said **you are** the light.
Your identity already carries radiance because His Spirit lives within you.
Radiating doesn't require perfection.
It requires presence, God's presence in you.

Your Light Isn't Loud, It's Transformational

Your light is not meant to overpower others.
Your light is meant to illuminate truth, love, and hope.
Your light shines when you
choose compassion over criticism
choose prayer over panic
choose peace over pressure
choose boundaries over burnout
choose forgiveness over bitterness
choose faith over fear
A woman who radiates God's presence changes the emotional temperature of every room she walks into.

Your Light Will Draw the Right People and Reveal the Wrong Ones

As you radiate God's transformation, your relationships will shift.
Some people will
feel comforted by your peace
feel strengthened by your faith
feel encouraged by your growth
feel inspired by your resilience
feel supported by your kindness
These are your people, the ones who walk beside you in purpose.
Others may
feel intimidated by your strength
feel resistant to your boundaries
feel frustrated by your healing

feel uncomfortable around your clarity
Do not dim your light for anyone.
Let your radiance reveal what God is aligning or removing.

Your Light Is Not Meant to Be Hidden

Fear may whisper
"I'm not ready."
"I'm not worthy."
"I don't want attention."
"I don't want to be judged."
"I don't want to step out."
But Jesus continues in Matthew 5:15–16,
"Let your light shine before others, that they may see your good deeds and glorify your Father in heaven."
Your light is not about you.
Your light is about Him.
God shines through your healed places.
God shines through your courage.
God shines through your gentleness.
God shines through your story.
God shines through your transformation.

Your Healing Becomes Someone Else's Hope

There is a woman who needs the wisdom you've gained.
There is a woman who needs the peace you now carry.
There is a woman who needs the strength you learned through surrender.
There is a woman who needs the story you once tried to hide.
There is a woman who will feel seen because of you.

You don't have to be perfect to help her.
You only need to be willing.
When you radiate God's light, you become part of someone else's healing.

A Truth to Hold Onto

A healed woman doesn't just rise; she radiates.
Her life becomes a living testimony of God's goodness, strength, and redemption.

Closing Prayer

Lord, help me radiate Your presence wherever I go. Let my life reflect Your love, peace, and strength. Use my healing as a light for others who are still searching for hope. Give me courage to shine, wisdom to guide, and compassion to uplift. Thank You for choosing me to carry Your light into the world. In Jesus' name, amen.

22

Redeemed – Embracing the Future God Is Preparing for You

There is a moment in every woman's journey when she realizes
My life is no longer defined by what broke me.
My future is no longer shaped by what wounded me.
My identity is no longer rooted in what I survived.
I am redeemed.
I am restored.
I am walking toward a future God Himself has prepared for me.

This chapter is your invitation to step forward without fear, without shame, and without the weight of old seasons. Redemption does not just heal the past. Redemption transforms the future.

You are not walking into the unknown alone.

You are stepping into a future held, guided, and blessed by God's hands.

Redemption Means Your Past Cannot Cancel Your Calling

Everything you have walked through — every mistake, every heartbreak, every season of confusion — is fully covered by grace.

Psalm 130:7 says,

"With the Lord is unfailing love and with Him is full redemption."

God does not partially redeem.

He fully restores.

He fully renews.

He fully reclaims the places the enemy tried to destroy.

Your story may have chapters you wish you could erase, but God uses every chapter as part of your calling.

Nothing about your past disqualifies you from your purpose.

Redemption Restores Your Identity

The enemy tried to name you

broken

unworthy

too much

too little

forgotten

unlovable

damaged

But God calls you

beloved

chosen

redeemed

renewed

restored
purposed
strengthened
His
Redemption is God rewriting your identity with truth.
You are not who you were yesterday.
You are who God says you are today.

Redemption Changes How You See Your Future

When you lived in survival, your future felt uncertain.
When you lived in fear, your future felt heavy.
When you lived in self-protection, your future felt risky.
But now that you have surrendered your past and renewed your mind, your future looks different.
You begin to see possibility instead of fear.
You begin to expect God's goodness instead of waiting for disappointment.
You begin to walk in confidence instead of caution.
You begin to believe the best is not behind you — **it is ahead of you.**
God is preparing a future that reflects His faithfulness, not your failures.

Redemption Restores What Was Lost

God specializes in restoring what you thought was gone forever.
Joy you thought would never return
Peace you thought you'd never feel again
Confidence you thought you'd lost
Purpose you thought you missed

Opportunities you thought were ruined
Relationships you thought were impossible
Dreams you thought were buried
Joel 2:25 declares,
"I will restore to you the years the locusts have eaten."
God does not merely repair what was damaged.
He returns it better.

Redemption Leads You Into Purpose

You are not here by accident.
You are not alive at this moment in history by coincidence.
There is a calling on your life — a purpose only you can fulfill.
Your healing was not just for you.
Your restoration was not just for your heart.
Your renewal was not just for your mind.
It was to prepare you to walk boldly in the purpose God lovingly crafted for you before the foundations of the world.
You have gifts inside you
voices waiting to be released
wisdom waiting to be shared
ideas waiting to be birthed
dreams waiting to be awakened
Your future is bigger than your fear.
Your calling is stronger than your past.

Redemption Frees You to Dream Again

Dreams buried by disappointment can live again.
Dreams hidden by insecurity can rise again.
Dreams suffocated by survival can breathe again.

Redemption is God whispering
"Daughter, it is safe to dream again."
You are free to hope.
Free to imagine.
Free to create.
Free to build.
Free to walk boldly into the life He designed for you.

Your Future Is Held by a Faithful God

You don't have to predict the future.
You don't have to control it.
You don't have to fear what is ahead.
You only need to trust the One who holds it.
Jeremiah 29:11 says,
"For I know the plans I have for you... plans to give you hope and a future."
Your future is secure.
Your future is protected.
Your future is blessed.
Your future is unfolding beautifully in God's timing.
You can walk forward with your head high and your heart steady.

A Truth to Hold Onto

Redemption means your past has no power, your present is full of purpose, and your future is held by a God who is faithful, loving, and good.

Closing Prayer

Lord, thank You for redeeming every part of my story. Thank You for restoring what I thought was lost and renewing what I thought was broken. Give me courage to step boldly into the future You've prepared for me. Help me trust Your plans, embrace Your calling, and walk forward with confidence, peace, and purpose. Redeem my dreams, my destiny, and every chapter ahead. In Jesus' name, amen.

Acknowledgments

Writing this book has been a journey of surrender, healing, and quiet obedience, one I could not have walked alone. I am deeply grateful to everyone who held space for me, prayed for me, encouraged me, and believed in what God was calling me to write.

To my family, thank you for your patience, your love, and your understanding when I needed quiet moments to write, pray, or breathe. Your support has been the steady ground beneath me. You are my heart, my joy, and my constant reminder of God's goodness.

To my friends who listened to my ideas, spoke life over me, and reminded me of what God placed inside me, thank you. Your encouragement helped me keep going on the days doubt tried to whisper louder than purpose.

To every woman who has ever walked through anxiety, battled silent fears, or carried more than she could confess, you inspired these pages. You are braver than you know, stronger than you feel, and more loved than you realize.

To the women who will read this book in quiet bedrooms, busy kitchens, parked cars, early mornings, or late at night, thank you for allowing me to walk with you. I am honored to be a small part of your renewal.

And above all, to my Lord and Savior, thank You for every word, every moment of clarity, every gentle nudge, and every breath of peace. This book exists because You renew, You restore, and You never leave us to carry life alone. All glory belongs to You.

Author's Note

If you have made it to this page, I want to pause and honor the journey you've walked through these chapters. Writing this book was a step of obedience for me, reading it was a step of courage for you.

I didn't write these words from a place of perfection or from a life free of anxiety or uncertainty. I wrote them from experience, from compassion, and from the same grace that God continues to pour into my own mind and heart. I wrote them as a woman who knows what it feels like to carry too much, think too hard, and struggle silently with the weight of thoughts that felt louder than truth.

But I also wrote them as a woman who has tasted God's peace, deeply, unexpectedly, and in ways I never thought possible.

My prayer is that somewhere in these pages, something shifted for you.
  Maybe it was a new perspective.
  Maybe it was a gentle conviction.
  Maybe it was a moment of clarity.
  Maybe it was the courage to finally let something go.

Whatever it was, I pray you carry it with you.

Renewal is not a one-time experience.

It's a daily walk, a rhythm of surrender, peace, and trust.

There will be days when your mind feels calm and steady, and days when old thoughts try to creep back in. That does not mean you've failed. It simply means you return to the practices you've learned:

Release again.
Rest again.
Renew again.
Rewrite again.
Reframe again.
Rise again.

And you will, because God is renewing you daily.

Thank you for letting me speak into your life, your mind, and your heart. Thank you for trusting me with your tender places. Thank you for opening these pages with the hope of something better, freer, and lighter.

I am praying for you.

I am cheering for you.

And I believe with my whole heart that God will continue the good work He began in you, one surrendered moment at a time.

All my love and blessings,
Liz

A Final Blessing Prayer

May the peace of God settle over your mind like a gentle covering, softening every anxious thought and quieting every storm within you.

May the Holy Spirit guide your steps, steady your heart, and whisper truth into the places where fear once lived.

May you walk with a renewed sense of confidence, not in your own strength, but in the God who holds you, leads you, and fights for you.

May every burden you once carried be replaced with a deeper trust, every lie you once believed be replaced with truth, and every place you once felt overwhelmed be filled with God's calm.

May you rise each day with clarity, move through each moment with grace, and rest each night knowing you are fully seen, fully loved, and fully held by the One who renews your mind and restores your soul.

May your thoughts align with His voice, your words reflect His goodness, and your life overflow with His peace.

And may you always remember: you are not alone, you are not behind, and you are not without hope. God is renewing you, day by day, moment by moment, thought by thought.

In Jesus' name, amen.

www.ingramcontent.com/pod-product-compliance
Lightning Source LLC
Chambersburg PA
CBHW020824150626
46554CB00018B/1916